WHAT IS MY PURPOSE?

8 SIMPLE STEPS TO FIND YOUR PURPOSE AND LIVE A LIFE YOU LOVE

SIMON FOSTER

TABLE OF CONTENTS

INTRODUCTION

"Efforts and courage are not enough without purpose and direction." John F. Kennedy

THERE IS MUCH TRUTH IN this quote from President Kennedy as without purpose, we tend to drift throughout life, never seeing our dreams become reality. Knowing your purpose in life is not some new age belief or only something saved for the religious or enlightened. Anyone can learn what their purpose in life is with just a few simple steps.

First it is important to understand what is meant by a purpose in life. There are many different interpretations of what that means. For the very religious, it may mean a calling from God. However, there is much more to a life purpose than what many connect to religion. A life purpose applies to everyone, whether your beliefs lean toward religion, non-religion or even atheism.

For some, using terms like life mission or purpose statement are preferred, yet they mean the same thing. However, feel free to use any terminology you wish that makes you comfortable as you begin taking the steps to know what your life mission, purpose statement, life direction or purpose in life may be.

Knowing your life purpose is the first step toward living a truly conscious life. A life purpose provides us with a clear goal, a set finish line that you truly want to reach. Without a clear vision of your life purpose, you could be working for 10, 20 or 30 years only to reach a goal you didn't want to reach.

"If the ladder is not leaning against the right wall, every step we take just gets us to the wrong place faster," Stephen R. Covey has been quoted as saying. If you are not aware of your life purpose, your goals and tasks may take you to a place where you don't want to be. You may know people who spent years earning degrees in higher education only to realize once they began working in that field that they hated it. These are people who did not take the time to learn their higher purpose before they began setting their goals.

Knowing your life purpose provides you with clarity of what you want driving you in this world. This allows you to set long-term goals that motivate you, short-term goals that will bring you closer to your long-term goals and action plans that will help you begin achieving those short-term goals. Without your clear life purpose, you will develop random goals and action plans, constantly spending your time busy with the agendas of those who have developed a clear action plan.

In today's busy world, people tend to get caught up with things that do not make a difference in their lives. You may feel you have to do things because society says you need to do those things, and, although some of the things that society deems important may be important in your life plan, they may not be as important to you as you thought once you determine what your life purpose is.

Knowing your life purpose gives your decisions meaning. Instead of spending 20 years in a job you hate, you can begin taking the steps to move toward a career that better fits your life purpose. Your life purpose may not be all that different from the job you are doing now, but it may be just different enough that you are not fulfilling your destiny in your current position. It may mean additional education or it could be a totally different career path. Until you see where a path takes you, it will be more difficult to know if you are taking the right one.

Finding what your life purpose is doesn't mean you need to uproot your life and make drastic changes. Changes can be made gradually at the pace that makes you the most comfortable. However, before you can begin taking those steps, you need to identify what your life purpose is in order to know what changes you need to make.

These eight steps can help you understand what your life purpose is in order for you to begin taking the steps necessary to achieve all your goals and dreams.

STEP 1 – LOOK WITHIN YOURSELF

TOO OFTEN, WE LOOK OUTSIDE ourselves when we search for what we think is important in our lives. Too often, we ignore the thing inside us that pulls us. You may wonder why some people seem to be able to pursue a passion from birth and you wonder why you were not born with that strong desire to do something. The fact is that you were born with that desire that pull you to be or do something. Unfortunately, too many of us do not listen to that voice inside of us telling us what we want to do, but listen to the ones that tell us what we should do.

EXTERNAL THINGS WILL NOT FULFILL YOU

The first step in finding your life purpose is to do a little digging inside yourself. Your inner self has the answers you are seeking, not those outside forces that try to push you toward other goals and dreams. Instead of looking toward external things to make you happy, understand that it is not external things that fulfill us, but those we hold inside ourselves that will guide us toward a successful outcome.

Too often, people think owning a nicer car or a bigger house will fulfill their needs. Some see a bigger paycheck as their purpose in life or finding the perfect mate will make them complete. Although being healthy is important to our well-being, having a flatter stomach or larger biceps is probably not our life purpose. Although it is important to challenge yourself, the time in your next marathon or what place you end up in the next competition is not your life purpose. Although reaching a particular time in a marathon or winning a big championship may seem like your life mission, what happens when you achieve that? Do you quit? More than likely you set the next goal and the next in order to keep motivated.

In order to know your true life mission, you must look deep inside yourself. Remember that no matter how much money you make, no matter how many things of value you have, external things do not bring fulfillment unless you have fulfilled your inner needs.

YOUR INNER SELF IS A REFERENCE BOOK

Look at your inner self as your reference book. It knows what your inner purpose is, but it is up to you to search through the information inside you to find it. Just as a reference book provides you with information about subjects, your inner self can provide you with the information you need to learn what your life purpose truly is.

Outside forces have a strong influence on how we listen to our inner self. As children, we hear people tell us what we should and should not do. We listen to the opinions, desires and expectations of others, whether they are parents, teachers or other people of influence. As we mature, we begin to replace our own opinions, desires and expectations with those we hear from the outside, losing the reference point in our inner self about how we truly feel and what we actually desire.

As a child, you may have told your parents that you wanted to be an actor. The initial reaction from the majority of parents would be to discourage a child from such a career because they know how difficult being successful in the acting world can be. As you grew older, you began to see that your parents were right and determined that you needed a career that was more stable. Yet, acting may still be your life purpose. The good news is that there are many careers that use acting talents that are not related to the stage or screen. Public speakers, attorneys, even salespeople use acting abilities to convey their message.

Dig deep into the reference book that is your inner self to remember what it was that you dreamed about when you were young. In all probability, your life purpose is connected to that childhood dream. You just need to find where it is filed in your inner self.

YOU CANNOT RUSH THE OUTCOME

Patience is an important part of searching your inner self. The answers to your questions cannot be rushed and if you attempt to force them, you will be unsuccessful. Look to the external world to confirm your internal thoughts. The purity of your mind is the only thing keeping the universe from telling you what you want to know.

Keep in mind that the creative energy will answer your questions about your life purpose as long as you give it time.

Understand that it is never too late to regain sight of your life purpose. Ray Kroc was 52 years old when he opened the first McDonald's. Harland "Colonel" Sanders was 65 when he opened his first Kentucky Fried Chicken. Both men tried living someone else's life purpose for many years before they discovered what theirs truly was. Mr. Kroc worked as a waiter, jazz pianist and traveling salesman before discovering what he was meant to do while Colonel Sanders quietly developed a fried chicken recipe that has gone on to become one of the best-selling fast food items in the world. The number of people who found their life purpose late in life is endless, proving that you are never too old to learn what your purpose in life actually is.

STILL YOUR MIND FOR THE ANSWERS

In order to dig deep into your inner self to find what your life purpose may be, sit in a comfortable position and focus on slowing your breathing. Focus on your breath as long as you can and push all thoughts out of your mind. When you mind is completely still, ask what your life's purpose is. It may take several days for your mind to become still enough for you to ask the question so be sure you do not ask until your mind is completely still.

Deduction vs. Induction

Once your mind is still, begin the process of deduction and induction. Deduction allows you to narrow down the field in order to determine where your passion lies. Induction uses things you have enjoyed doing in the past to determine if there is a consistent theme in what you enjoy. By using both deduction and induction, you can narrow the field of possibilities to things you enjoyed doing in the past. Using the two together works best as you could spend years trying new things to see if you have a passion for them when, in all honesty, what you enjoy is more than likely something you have done before.

The first step is to narrow it down to the point you have deduced what made you happy in the past. What were you passionate about when you were a child? A young teen? A young adult? Go try some of those things. If you were passionate about writing, take a creative writing course to see if you still enjoy it. Or simply sit down and start writing – you may begin the next bestselling novel. If the passion is no longer there, deduce something else that you used to be passionate about and try that. Keep trying until the passion is rekindled. In most cases, the first thing you try ends up being your life purpose, but if it does not, keep trying until you feel that passion rekindle inside you again. When you don't feel the passion, return to your stilled mind to see where you may direct your path to the thing that creates the most passion in your life.

DIFFERENTIATE PURPOSE FROM GOALS

It is important to remember that purpose and goals are not the same thing. Goals are a specific endpoint that guides your behavior. Purpose is broader and may stimulate the goals you need to set in order to achieve that purpose. It is better to look at purpose as you do values. There may not be a terminal outcome as there is in goals.

Let's look at that marathon time again. A goal may be to run that marathon in less than two hours. That means that the time you achieve is not your purpose. The purpose may be to simply complete every marathon you undertake. Instead, the time you want to complete the marathon is a goal. Once you have achieved that goal, you will probably set another one, but your purpose will not change. Your purpose is still to run marathons and complete them.

STEP 2 – UNDERSTAND OUTSIDE FORCES

ONCE YOU HAVE ASKED YOUR inner self what your life's purpose is, it is time to look outside yourself to confirm what you have discovered. Although determining your life's purpose comes from within, living that purpose requires attention to outside forces as well.

When we say that external forces have an effect on our life purpose, it does not mean that those external forces change what your purpose in life is. External forces have little bearing on our happiness, despite the fact that many people equate "things" with being happy.

In reality, outside forces provide us with short-term happiness rather than with long-term happiness. Look at lottery winners whose money is all gone after a few years or celebrities who seek solace in drugs or alcohol despite their fame and fortune.

These are people who thought things would bring them everything they desire in life. What they did not develop was the inner peace they needed to reach their life purpose. Although that singer with the drug addiction may have looked at a hit record as their life purpose, they focused more on the riches attached to that record than they did on the enjoyment of singing.

For these reasons, it is important to understand how outside forces can have a bearing on our life purpose. They can send us down a path we didn't intend to travel or may guide us completely away from what we know we were meant to do in life, whether because of financial obligations or the pressure of others. By being aware of and understanding these outside forces, we can counteract their influence on our purpose and keep us from straying too far from what our soul tells us we want to do.

PAYING ATTENTION WILL PROVIDE THE ANSWERS

One way to keep outside factors in balance with inner desires is to pay attention to the world around you. Nature and events often answer our questions regarding our life purpose, but we are sometimes too busy to notice what we are being told. In order to understand the answer, you must pay attention to things that are happening in your life. The universe provides us with clues, ideas and even outright answers to all of our questions, yet it is human nature to ignore what is presented clearly.

Suppose a friend asked you a question and then walked away from you before you answered. This is exactly what people do every day when they ask certain questions. Whether you are praying or simply asking the universe a question, do you wait for an answer? Do you pay attention to the signs being given to you? Or do you ask the question and then go on about your day? By stilling your mind when you ask, you should become sensitive to even subtle shifts around you. You will begin to notice things that make your decisions clearer. This is the universe shifting reality to push you into noticing what it is trying to tell you.

This is not something that will happen immediately as you search for your life purpose. As mentioned before, this will take time and patience. You may notice the changes gradually or suddenly realize that things are much clearer for you. If you are stressed or have inner turmoil, delay trying to understand outside forces until you can calm your mind because a mind in turmoil will not let you see the answer to your question.

DON'T ASK UNLESS YOU WANT TO LOOK FOR THE ANSWER

It is important to understand that your life purpose may be something completely different than you expected. Even if your chosen profession was one you desired even as a child, there may be something inside you that sees your life purpose in another direction.

Life does not follow a straight path although many people feel as if they must meet a series of milestones, in a particular order, in order to achieve complete happiness. They must graduate from high school, attend college, find a great job, get married, have children and retire – all in that order. The fact is that there is nothing written that says we must follow this straight-and-narrow path to get to our life purpose and there is also nothing wrong if this straight path does take us where we want to be.

Too often, teenagers leave high school and head directly to college with a life plan in hand. Once in college, they may realize that the program they entered is not making them happy. They realize they don't want a career in this chosen field after all. Yet, too many people simply continue on the path, ignoring their inner selves because it is "what I am supposed to do."

There is nothing wrong with backtracking in order to correct our direction in life. Have you ever been in the wrong relationship? Wasn't there a sense of relief when one of you finally realized it was wrong and ended it? There may have been pain initially, but, in the long run, you both realized that it was causing more damage staying together than it was being apart. You may make several wrong turns on the path to finding your life purpose, but like that relationship, you should pay attention to your inner self when it tells you what you are doing is wrong.

When you ask yourself what your purpose in life is, be prepared to hear something you were not expecting. You may learn that the job you have been doing for 30 years is actually not what you were meant to do. You may learn that all the money in the bank, nice cars in the driveway and the big house in the best neighborhood is not what you wanted. This could mean a significant change in your life and you must be prepared to hear things you may not want to hear.

However, never let your fears about what your inner self believes is your true life purpose to stop you from asking. You simply must be prepared for the answer which may initially be a surprise, but that deep down you knew all along.

WAIT FOR INNER HARMONY

It cannot be stressed enough that to find your true life purpose, you must have inner harmony. When you ask what your life purpose is, your mind must be clear of turmoil and stress. You must be at peace in order for the universe to show you where you need to be.

When you are at peace, you are able to see more of the world around you. When your mind is full of anger, guilt, fear or self-doubt, it affects how we view the world. Strength adds strength to the universe while weakness can actually weaken the world around us.

Have you ever been in a group of people when one of them became enraged? It may have been in a meeting or at a workshop you were attending when something was said they didn't like. Could you feel the anger take over the room? Could you sense toxic energy affecting everyone who was within the sound of their voice? The same thing happens when we let toxic thoughts take over our inner self.

When you begin to think of inner harmony as not just a way for you to reach happiness, but also as a way to keep the universe happy, you feel a greater responsibility for achieving that inner peace. Instead of looking at it as a selfish need on your own part, you begin to see it as an important factor in achieving peace on a greater level.

DOES IT SERVE OTHERS?

Initially, it may appear that our life purpose is for us and us alone with no impact on the world as a whole. The fact is that every life purpose will have improved the world in some way. It does not have to be on a global scale, but simply the world around you. An artist improves the world by adding beauty. An attorney helps those who are facing a complicated court system find justice. A nutritionist helps people live healthier lives so that they may enjoy their friends and family longer.

In ancient Samurai culture, death was worshipped every day. They believed that this gave people freedom and focus because if you are aware that you are going to die, you will enjoy every day as if it is your last. You are going to be more likely to help other people. You will want your work remembered. This belief is often confirmed by people who have a loved one who died young. They say that they learned from the death of the loved one that life is too short and that you must live each day as if there would be no tomorrow. This attitude freed them to do good works for others, to begin living their life purpose and to see how their actions impacted the world around them.

Do Not Let Outside Influences Dissuade You

When you first begin living your life purpose, you will more than likely meet resistance from outside forces, especially if your life purpose is drastically different from the life you are living. If you are a wealthy attorney who sees a need to help those who cannot afford your services, you may get resistance from business partners or a spouse. If you own a successful business and you are suddenly called to sell it in order to do mission work in a third-world country, outside forces will more than likely try to dissuade you from taking such drastic steps.

It is important to resist the attempts by those on the outside from doing what your inner self is calling you to do. It will be difficult, but in the long run, even the outside factors will see that you are doing what will make you happiest. In some cases, you may need to make those changes gradually in order to reduce the stress on a spouse or business partner, but you need to begin taking the steps necessary to begin living for your life purpose.

Although you need to keep the needs of your family and colleagues in mind, you cannot live someone else's life purpose but can only live the one meant for you.

STEP 3 – STEP OUT OF YOUR COMFORT ZONE

EVERYONE HAS THEIR OWN BUBBLE that they live in comfortably. It is the world where we surround ourselves with our friends, our job and our family. It is where we think we succeed and where we derive the most pleasure. In this small world, we are concerned only with our own pleasure and comfort, although we naturally have concerns for our close friends and family members. But it is also in this bubble where we develop the majority of the problems we have in life.

We are comfortable in this little world – hence the term "comfort zone." We don't have to exercise or eat healthy because we are comfortable there. We don't have to talk to strangers because everyone in this world is known to us. We can procrastinate, we don't have to tackle anything difficult, we know what to expect from those around us. So, you may ask, where is the problem?

The problem is that when we remain in our comfort zone, we only see things from a self-centered approach.

We don't develop skills to know when our actions are causing us problems. When someone says something negative around us, we immediately think it is about us because we have no reference outside the comfort zone to relate the comment to other than ourselves. We take no risks. We simply exist.

For this reason, in order to know what your life purpose is, you must step outside of our comfort zone.

YOU MAY EXCEL AT SOMETHING NEW

The most important benefit when you step outside your comfort zone is that you may find that you excel at something you didn't know you did. You may learn an artistic skill that has remained dormant for years or you may discover you have a talent for advising others in their life path. When you remain in your bubble, you don't take risks and you don't try new things, which mean you don't discover your true potential.

There is no question that stepping outside of your comfort zone is scary and far too many people in this world won't do it simply because it is frightening. You may have the next Pulitzer Prize winning novel in your head, but you won't sit down and begin putting it on paper because it is outside your comfort zone. Maybe you fear rejection from publishers or you think you won't ever finish it. You use the excuse you really can't write or that you are way too busy to write a book. This means you never discover your true potential because you simply don't try.

Let's analyze what can happen if your inner self is telling you to write that novel. The worst is that a publisher rejects it when you send it off. Stephen King's first novel, Carrie, was rejected 30 times. He became so disillusioned, he tossed it in the trash and his wife fished it out. John Grisham's first novel, A Time to Kill, was rejected 12 times and he attempted selling copies out of the trunk of his car. J.K. Rowling had Harry Potter and the Sorcerer's Stone rejected by dozens of publishers, only finding success after the eight-year-old daughter of a publisher read it and loved it. If your novel is rejected, you will not be alone. Every writer suffers from rejection at some point.

But those writers stepped out of their comfort zone and kept sending off those novels. In 2012, Stephen King earned $39 million. John Grisham earned $26 million. J.K. Rowling became the first author billionaire in history. If you step out of your comfort zone, you may achieve the success these authors did, but only if you take the risk and begin writing that novel.

NEVER BE AFRAID OF NEW THINGS

Fear of the unknown is the biggest reason most people do not try new things. People frequent the same restaurants over and over because they are familiar with the menu. They don't try new foods because they are afraid they will not like them. The live each day with a routine that never changes. People tend to stick to things where they feel safe and familiar. But when it comes to finding your life purpose, you need to be willing to try new things.

For many people, yoga or meditation may seem like new age practices full of incense and chanting. The idea of simply relaxing, breathing and quieting your mind may seem impossible and may actually feel uncomfortable doing them at first. They may be resistant to the benefits because it just feels unnatural to them. However, with practice, almost anyone who has tried yoga or meditation finds that it provides an inner peace they did not have before trying it. They are grateful that they found something that allows them to relax and feel the universe in ways they never had before.

Trying new things can be frightening but that doesn't mean you should resist them. As part of stepping out of your comfort zone, you will have to attempt things you have never attempted before. It is all the process toward finding your life purpose.

THE UNIVERSE TAKES YOU TO YOUR PERFECT DESTINATION

By searching for the purpose of your life in places you have never looked before, you open yourself up to the universe. The universe sees all that you do and once you have opened up your mind to new and exciting things, the universe will guide you down the path toward your life purpose. It will begin opening doors that were previously closed, creating new paths for you to follow as you move toward that purpose.

By being one with the universe, opportunities will surround you. In fact, many people who have followed these steps say that if felt as if they were flooded with opportunity once they opened their mind to their inner self and to the universe around them.

Inspiration Comes from Everywhere

The universe even provides you with signs for what new things you need to try in order to achieve your life purpose. Look around you for inspiration. A simple conversation with a friend could lead to an idea related to your purpose. A magazine article about a successful person may provide you with insight into the things you should try.

Opportunity surrounds you from the minute you hit the alarm clock in the morning until you doze off with a book on your chest at night. It is the seed that inspires daydreams and evenings lying on the grass looking up at the stars. Opportunity does not come in one color or shape nor does it appear at times when you are looking for it. A networking event at a local chamber of commerce can be an opportunity to connect with your best future client. A ride on a country road could reveal the opportunity to buy your dream house. A quick visit to the grocery store could result in meeting the love of your life.

Many people call these occurrences "fate" or "luck." They think this all happens by chance. The fact is that the universe guides you to these events, locations or people in order for you to achieve your life purpose. It is up to us to make the most of the opportunities, however, which is why it is critical to be in tune with the universe so that we do not miss the chances that are provided to us.

DO NOT OPERATE IN SLEEP MODE

How many times have you driven to work and not even remembered driving there? Have you ever been sitting at your desk staring out the window and been asked what you are thinking, only to have no answer? During this time you may be operating in sleep mode, a time when you are living in your imagination. It is during this time when life just happens and you may not even realize what you are doing. It may come to light when you catch yourself saying "I can't believe I just did that."

During these times we are not centered in our true self and are moving through life mechanically. The more awake we become, the more inspired our actions are so that you create a magnetic center that integrates us. Energy flows through our being so that self-contradicting thoughts that keep us from seeing our true life purpose vanish. We are aligned with a higher self and a higher purpose without the negative thoughts that sabotage our efforts to reach our life purpose.

As you step out of your comfort zone, you may actually find yourself falling into sleep mode less often, because you are doing things that stretch you mentally and physically, you will focus more and be less likely to allow your mind to drift.

Keep in mind that there is nothing wrong with daydreaming. Daydreaming is an excellent way to connect with your inner self, but when you daydream without purpose, you may find yourself drifting, performing duties that are not moving you toward your life purpose. Therefore, convert daydreaming to creative visualization and you will find yourself achieving far more in your life.

DO MORE THINGS THAT CHALLENGE YOU

One thing that stepping out of your comfort zone does is to activate your creativity. Far too many people find creativity a risky venture. When you share something that is creative, you risk rejection and this makes you vulnerable. However, risking failure opens us up to greater achievements. In fact, the more often that you step out of your comfort zone the more likely it is you will do it again.

As you open yourself up to new experiences, you will discover more qualities that relate to your purpose in life, whether it is curiosity, imagination or interests you never knew you had. You cultivate openness to experimentation and learn that even failure can be a learning experience.

There is also evidence that new challenges can help you age better. A 2013 study found that learning new and demanding skills can help you stay mentally sharp as you get older. As we age, mental acuity can diminish but researchers have found that those who continuously challenge their mental capacity showed better mental acuity than those who were not challenged.

Of course, you don't want to step so far out of your comfort zone to the point that you become stressed. As we have already discussed, stress can keep you from finding the inner peace you need to find the answers you seek. If you find yourself stressed or unable to concentrate when attempting new things, step back and think about what it is that is causing the stress. You may need to choose a task that is slightly less stressful. For example, if deciding to run a marathon is causing you stress, consider building up to the long race with shorter ones to build endurance and eliminate fears.

STEP 4 – KNOW YOUR HIGHER SELF

THE NEXT STEP IN FINDING your purpose in life is to know your higher self. Being in though with our higher self will not only help the universe respond to our questions, but will also open up our minds to seeing what the universe is trying to tell us. As mentioned before, we often miss opportunities because we have not connected with our higher self and are unable to see what is right before our eyes.

RELAX AND BECOME OBSERVANT

The first step in connecting to our higher self is to relax. We cannot reach our higher being if we are thinking about the tasks we have to do the next day, the chores that need doing around the house or the numbers that need crunching for that report due on Friday.

Sit back, relax and observe. Pay attention to details and nudges from the universe. If you are relaxed, the universe will respond to the questions you have asked. Relaxation brings us closer to our higher being so that we may see more of what is available to us.

In fact, one of the best times to connect with your higher self is just before you get ready to fall asleep. Just as you are dozing off at night, ask yourself what your life's purpose is, then, without allowing another thought into your head, let you fall asleep.

DREAMS HOLD ANSWERS

Because the subconscious is quick to respond when you pose a question just before falling asleep, the answer to your question may come in the form of a symbolic dream. There are many studies that indicate that dreams may give us insight into our higher self.

When we meditate on dreams, those that may not make sense at first glance may become clearer. Some experts believe that the dream state is a method the brain uses to provide us with insight into ourselves. Some believe that when we dream about others, they are our spirit guides disguised as people we know who are leading us toward our purpose in life.

When you wake up in the morning, immediately write down your dream. Try to be as detailed as possible and then watch what happens around you throughout the day. You may notice some of what happened in the dream is closely connected to what happens to you throughout the day. This is a sign that your higher self is connecting with you through your dreams and will guide you to your purpose in life.

There are other methods you can use besides analyzing your dreams that may help you learn more about your life purpose. There are different methods because the approaches work differently for different people. The best thing to do is to look over all of them and choose the one that looks like would work best for you.

WORD ASSOCIATION EXERCISE

In this exercise, think about the question of finding your life's purpose. Do not think about anything else but this question and focus on it completely. Open a book or magazine that is nearby. Close your eyes and open any page and point at the page. Open your eyes and write down the word that you chose. Do the same thing, choosing words on different pages four more times until you have written five words on the paper.

For this exercise to work, you must be connected to your higher self. Your subconscious will use the words in the book to present you with clues regarding your life's purpose because your conscious mind is not interrupting.

Look at the words you selected and connect them to find your life's purpose. For example, the words had, grow, life, age, experience could be interpreted as "I have to grow (develop myself) all my life and share my experiences with others."

It may take a little creative thinking and reviewing to determine what the words you have chosen may mean, but by clearing your mind and letting your subconscious guide you, the meaning will become clear.

THE VENN DIAGRAM

The Venn Diagram is based on the idea that your life purposes is something you enjoy doing, something you are good at and something that improves the lives of others. However, in order to determine your life purpose, you must dig deeper than those surface ideas. In this technique, you choose one of the three ideas to start with. It is recommended that you do not start with things that make the world a better place because the term is too broad to fit into your life at first.

Once you have chosen either things you are good at or thing you enjoy doing, write down everything that falls under that category. Remember that you are only focusing on one of them at a time. Include everything you can think of, no matter how trivial it may seem. If you are writing things you enjoy doing, you may include sitting in the sunshine, petting your dog, writing short stories or fishing. Do not try to think realistically as this shuts down the creative process. Even if the things you enjoy doing are unrealistic, such as taking a cruise or traveling around the world, include them in the list.

Once you think you have written everything down you enjoy doing or that you do well, ask others for input. They may remind you of something you have forgotten. A friend may remind you that you enjoyed getting a pedicure or that you enjoyed helping a child learn to read. Add those to the list as well. When you think you have everything on the list, give yourself five minutes, sitting in front of the paper, thinking even more. If you have not come up with more items to add to the list in five minutes, move on to the next step.

Look at the list and narrow them down based on the other two areas. If you wrote a list regarding what you enjoy doing, note which of the items on that list are something you are also good at. Once you have done that, look over the matching items to see which you could use to make the world a better place.

You will know when the item on the list is right because you will feel excitement when you see it, you will feel motivated and begin thinking of ways that you can begin applying steps in your life to make it happen. You will have a clear vision of what your life purpose is.

THE EXHAUSTIVE LIST TECHNIQUE

The Exhaustive List Technique is much like the brainstorming done in the business world. Use a large piece of blank paper and write at the top "What is my life purpose?" You then write down everything that pops in your head. Don't think about what you are writing or ignore a thought that pops in your head. Write everything down, even if the thought makes no sense.

As you keep writing, you will begin to notice that some seem to stick with you more than others. You will catch yourself coming up with related thoughts. Be sure to write them down as well. Continue writing until you have exhausted every thought and then switch to another area of your life where your life purpose might lie.

As you write, you will eliminate daily thoughts on the topic and begin to feel resistance. You will want to stop, but don't. When you reach a point when you think you have no more thoughts, take a deep breath and relax your mind. Breathe deeply, but don't force thoughts into your head. Let them come naturally. As you push past the resistance, you force your thoughts deeper. You begin to see the things that are truly important in your life and what your higher self really wants you to see.

This may not come easily to you. It could take as much as 20 minutes to get all your thoughts out on paper. For some people, it may take an hour or two to get past the surface level of thought. However, once you dig down into what is truly important, you can begin to see where your life purpose may be. You may become emotional as you see the things that matter the most to you on paper. It may be that the thoughts that make you emotional are strongly connected to your life purpose.

Once you write down your life purpose, you will know. You will feel a strong surge of emotion at one of the thoughts you write down. When that happens, you have discovered your purpose in life.

THE WOUND OF WISDOM DISCIPLINE

The Wound of Wisdom Discipline is based on the theory that many ancient tribes believed – that wisdom enters the warrior through wounds. In these cultures, boys would cut themselves deeply and fill them with ash which left obvious scars. They believed that these scars were signs of wisdom as they grew into manhood.

When we face adversity in life, scars are left behind. Although these scars may not be visible, they helped us grow into who we are today. In most cases, we learn from the adversity we faced, giving us the wisdom that the ancient warriors believed physical scars provided. When using the Wound of Wisdom Technique, ask yourself:

* What big adversity have I overcome in my life?

* How can I help others do the same?

This technique works for those who have a desire to help others after facing adversity of their own. If you are not interested in helping others who have suffered similar problems in their past through coaching, inspirational talks or other methods, this technique may not provide you with the answers you are seeking. For those who have overcome drug or alcohol addiction, or have been the victim of abuse, this technique may guide them toward helping others who may be suffering from the same adversity.

THE EULOGY TECHNIQUE

The Eulogy Technique requires you to look into the future. You imagine yourself five or ten years in the future, picturing how your life would look if you changed nothing. For many people, this leads to a moment when you realize your future is not going to be what you desire, so you need to make changes now to prevent that from happening. In order to use this technique, you look even further into the future, literally all the way to the end of your life as you lie on your deathbed. Imagine that everything went the way you wanted in your life. Ask yourself the following questions:

> * Who is by your side as you lie on your deathbed?

> * What will you say to them?

> * What will they say to you?

> * What do you wish you had achieved in your lifetime?

* What are your fondest memories?

Think about the answers to those questions as they will provide you with insight into what you really find important and may show you some surprising things that you thought were important that actually are not. Bring your thoughts back to the future and sum up the entire exercise in one phrase. That phrase will be your life purpose.

Understand that your life may end up being completely different from what you envision. There is nothing wrong with that because this exercise is designed to show you what is important to you now, not what is important in the future. It allows you to discover what you find inspiring and motivating now in order to achieve your dreams.

These techniques, whether you choose one of them or a combination of different methods, can help guide you even closer to your purpose in life. Now it is time to take the steps toward documenting what you have learned through the techniques you have used. One of the best ways to do this is through journaling.

STEP 5 – JOURNALING

JOURNALING IS ONE OF THE MOST critical things to do when you are searching for your purpose in life. Journaling is an ancient tradition as evidence of writing in journals has been found as far back as 10th century Japan. Throughout history, journals have provided insight into historical events, beliefs and the thoughts of some of the most famous people in the world.

"I never travel without my diary," said Oscar Wilde, a 19th century playwright. "One should always have something sensational to read on the train." Journals and diaries have always had a sensational reputation, as a way for people to record their inner most thoughts. The diary of a teenaged girl is often hidden and guarded from the prying eyes of others.

Journaling provides us with significant health benefits with some research indicating that it may improve our immune system. Other studies have found that journaling reduces symptoms of asthma and rheumatoid arthritis. It is thought that writing about events that are stressful may reduce the impact of them on your health.

Journaling helps you clarify your thoughts and feelings as well as help you get to know yourself better. By putting your anger, stress or frustrations on paper, you feel calmer and the feelings become less intense. People tend to solve problem from an analytical perspective, but sometimes using creativity and intuition has more of an impact on solving problems than analytical study. In addition, journaling can resolve conflict as it can help you see someone else's point of view.

However, journaling can also help you determine what your purpose in life is. Your written words can be a guide to your inner most thoughts which, in turn, can answer the question of what your life purpose truly is.

20-Day Diary

Journaling does not have to be extensive in order to be therapeutic. In fact, within 20 days of journaling, you can get a better focus on what your life purpose is. Although it is recommended that journaling be a lifelong process, by keeping a 20-day journal to start, you can begin to see a pattern in your thought process that may guide you toward what your life purpose is.

For 20 days, write down everything that happens in your life, no matter how trivial it may seem, and the feelings you had during those times. Be honest and frank. At the end of the 20 days, read the journal as if it was the newest best seller you picked up at the bookstore. Search for patterns and activities where you felt happiness, joy or excitement.

Once you have read over your diary, talk to your friends. Ask them to provide you with a visual of you as they see you. Note their responses and then compare them to what your journal says about you. Are there any things in common? If you find that your friends see the same qualities in you as your journal, it is most likely your life purpose.

ADMIRATION OF OTHERS TELLS YOU ABOUT YOURSELF

Think about the qualities of someone else that you admire. Do you admire the courage of a cancer patient? The intelligence of a college professor? The tenacity of someone who has survived tremendous adversity? The fact is that the qualities you admire in those people are probably qualities that exist within you as well.

This is why it is important to get feedback from others regarding how they visualize you and why you need to understand what qualities you are attracted to in your life. Often, people with similar qualities will attract each other. Too often, however, we attribute those qualities to others but do not attribute them to ourselves when they more than likely are just as prominent within us as they are others.

Knowing what others admire in you can help guide you to your life purpose as well. Those qualities are an underlying guide to what is important in your life. If we leave those qualities hidden in our unconscious, we always look to others for guidance rather than accessing our own inner resources. This can cause us to lose sight of our purpose in life as we attach that purpose to others rather than ourselves.

LIFE'S PURPOSE AND HEREDITY

Your family tree can also tell you a lot about your life purpose. Many people who have researched their family tree have found common life purposes throughout history. It may be teaching, leading others or the need to heal, but often there is a common thread of purpose in life in families.

As part of your journaling, begin noting who your ancestors were, what they were interested in, what they did in life in order to see how history has a bearing on what you find important. If the career of your great-great-great grandmother connects with some of the things you have journaled, you may have a genetic propensity for that same type of career. That may be a clear indication of what your life purpose is.

STEP 6 – DO THINGS YOU ENJOY

BY NOW, YOU HAVE DETERMINED what your life purpose is, but what do you do with it once you have discovered it? For some, even after they discover what the purpose in life is, it is difficult to understand what it means in the long run. The fact is that you don't have to worry about saving the entire world. As the Childlike Empress in the Neverending Story says to the main character, Bastian, "Just follow your wishes one by one, as they come, and they will eventually lead you down the right path."

Although the quote is from a work of fiction, real life works in exactly the same way. It is rare for anyone to have a clearly defined life purpose, but because it makes for good stories, it is what most people have come to expect. They have unrealistic expectations of what they are able to do. Instead, they need to focus on what they enjoy and do as much of it as they can until what they enjoy intertwines with what makes them happy.

SHORT-TERM ENJOYMENT VS. LONG TERM SATISFACTION

It is important to understand that there is a difference between doing things you enjoy in the short-term and doing things you enjoy in the long-term. Although they may be similar, that may not always be the case. You may enjoy eating an entire pizza in the short-term, but in the long-term you regret that decision.

The fact is that working on your life purpose may not always be pleasant. In fact, there are times that it may be extremely difficult. Suppose you have decided to start your own business. To do so, you may need to leave a job that has provided you with financial security. It may mean that until your business grows, you have to reduce your spending. You must eliminate a few dinners at your favorite restaurant or walk past those new shoes that are calling your name. In the short-term, those sacrifices are hard, but the long-term satisfaction of owning your own business is far more fulfilling than those shoes or a steak dinner.

LIVING WITH PASSION

There are three basic cornerstones to living with passion:

* Fundamentals of living with passion

* Aligning your core values

* Finding your life purpose

We have covered methods for finding your life purpose, but let's look at the other two aspects of living with passion.

The fundamentals of living with passion include taking care of your body, managing your energy levels and practicing self-awareness. If you do not take care of your physical and mental state or are not aware of things going on in your life, your passion may dwindle. Although being mentally and physically healthy may not seem like fun things to do, they are very useful in kindling your passion for life.

ALIGNING YOUR CORE VALUES

Your core values are what guides you through life. Going against your core values is like attempting to swim upstream. It makes life harder and you quickly lose the passion for getting to your destination. When you go with your core values, it is much easier to float down that stream and the trip to your destination is much more pleasant.

Core values are different for everyone and may include freedom, security, family, honesty, peace and even power. You may have similar core values to others, but they will not be in the same order of importance or of equal value.

Aligning your core values is important when you are establishing your life purpose as they must complement each other. Just like swimming upstream, you may reach your destination, but you will have a better chance at getting there if you work with the river rather than against it.

Take Action

Doing nothing will not only keep you from learning what your purpose in life is, it can also keep you from achieving many of your goals. You can sit at home and watch television rather than going to the gym. You can skip the networking event because you'd rather read a book. But in doing so, you do not take action and your life purpose will remain elusive.

This does not mean you have to do things you don't enjoy doing, but remember that you must challenge yourself if you want to find your life purpose. Find a gym where you can watch television when you work out. Ask a friend to attend the mixer with you. There are ways to get around your discomfort and still find your life purpose.

Relax But Don't Stop

Once you have discovered your purpose in life, you can relax, but don't stop working toward it. Remember that your goals are the path you will take toward your purpose in life. Your purpose in life is also the guiding factor for the goals you choose. They are all intertwined so although you can relax once you know where your purpose in life lies, you must continue the process in order to achieve fulfillment.

Step 7 – Choose the Right Transition

ALL THE STEPS DISCUSSED PREVIOUSLY are meant to help you discover your life purpose. During these steps it is okay to think crazy and not be realistic. Once you have discovered your passion, however, you need to come back to reality. It is now time to transition from your current life to one that follows your life purpose.

As much as we would like life to be like fiction, it is not realistic to quit your job, sell your house and drive off into the sunset with your dog in a basket to pursue your life purpose. Instead, you must transition into living a purposeful life.

The Main Job Transition

If your job already relates to your life passion, you can begin living a more purposeful life by eliminating tasks that you don't enjoy and replacing them with things that you do. If you work for yourself, you can begin to outsource the things you don't enjoy as you grow more successful. You can hire someone to do your accounting or a personal assistant to answer the phone. You can hire sales people to bring in more customers. By learning what your life purpose is, you may find that your business becomes more successful, allowing you to outsource more of the work and focus on what makes you happy.

If you work for someone else, it may be more difficult to eliminate tasks you don't enjoy. Because you are following your passion, you will be good at what you do so that your company sees how valuable you are. This could mean a promotion or the ability to request tasks you enjoy while delegating those you do not. If your company is not willing to allow you to delegate tasks or does not see your value, consider changing to a company that will.

THE SIDE JOB TRANSITION

When your current job is not related to your life purpose, you may need to transition to one that does on a gradual basis. In this scenario, continue working at your present job and begin developing your life purpose outside of work. As your passion grows, you can slowly diminish your time at your current job to spend more time on what makes you happy until you can quit the first job completely.

This is the perfect option for those who have a passion for something they can do just a few hours per week to begin. Artists, writers or other creative individuals can begin working in their spare time on their craft, building clientele to the point they can begin doing what they love full time. This is also the method used when you need additional training in order to live your life purpose. If you have the desire to become a nurse or doctor, you may need to further your education. You can begin taking steps to do that on a part-time basis as well.

THE JUST LEAP TRANSITION

For some people, the best method to transition to a purposeful life is to simply just leap into it 100 percent. They may actually quit their job, sell their house and load their dog in a basket, heading off into the sunset. Although this is one of the most exciting things to do, it is also the most risky as it may take some time for your life purpose to support you.

First, you need to make sure you can support yourself. Try to save at least six months of salary as it could take that long, if not longer, to sustain yourself with your life purpose. Despite the fact that this is a risky proposition, it may be better than spending your life in a job that no longer fulfills your inner self, but only provides you with material comforts which we know are not fulfilling.

If you don't have six months of salary saved or it is difficult for you to save money, there are steps you can take to live a purposeful life. Begin developing skills in your life purpose, read books that provide you with guidance and make the changes necessary that will help you move into a position that will allow you to make the leap necessary to fulfill your life purpose.

THE ETERNAL SIDE JOB

For some people, their life purpose will not lead to a full-time job, although that is extremely rare. It is possible that your purpose in life cannot sustain you financially. It could be that you discover your life purpose is taking care of your family but also helping to improve the lives of others. You may not be able to stay at home with your children due to financial reasons, but you could spend the majority of your time with them and seek a side job that allows you to help others as well.

However, do not use the eternal side job as an excuse not to live your life purpose. It is very rare that your life purpose cannot become something that supports you financially. Therefore, before settling for the eternal side job, dig deep within you to be sure that other options are not available.

Step 8 – Recognize When You Have Multiple Purposes

It is possible that you may have more than one life purpose. However, it is important to remember that multiple life purposes often reduce resources for each purpose. If you are pursuing one life purpose, it is easy to become disheartened by obstacles placed in your way. If you are trying to pursue multiple purposes, does allow you to shift resources to a purpose that may be more feasible. However, too many purposes can lead to constant shifting of resources so that no progress is made on any one purpose.

Three Dimensions of Purpose

It is important to remember that there are three dimensions of purpose as you look within to determine what your life purpose is. Scope dictates how action is influenced and purposes have an impact on all actions. Thoughts or emotions should have a broad scope. A broad scope will be less organized but will have an impact on a wider range of behaviors.

A purpose with a broad but strong scope should have more of an effect on outcomes and will bring about resiliency when obstacles appear. By creating a broad, strong purpose, you are more likely to create stronger structural frameworks.

Awareness is important as you must be aware of your purpose and be able to articulate what that purpose is. Awareness is what motivates you to live your life purpose. When someone is not aware of their life purpose, they may still be influenced by it, but they will not attribute the resources necessary to behave in such a way that their life purpose can be revealed

.

Conclusion

By following these simple steps, you can determine what your purpose in life is and learn how to transition your current life into one that leads to a more purposeful life.

I hope you enjoyed this book as much as I enjoyed writing it.

ABOUT THE AUTHOR

Simon Foster is a Master of Education, professional Interpreter and Translator and Kindle Publisher Author.

He loves educating and inspiring people to succeed and live the life of their dreams.

ONE LAST THING...

If you enjoyed this book or found it useful I'd be very grateful if you'd post a short review on Amazon. Your support really does make a difference and I read all the reviews personally so I can get your feedback and make this book even better.

Thanks again for your support!

BONUS CHAPTER

HOW TO BE HAPPY - 10 EASY WAYS TO LIVE A HAPPIER LIFE

CHAPTER 1 - WHY IT'S SO IMPORTANT TO BE HAPPY

By now, everyone is familiar with the notion that stress and unhappiness can lead to negative health conditions. The biological impact on the brain and other major organs caused by stress and unhappiness can lead to chronic heart disease, strokes and diabetes. An overall lack of happiness can lead to a negative view of the world and a person's place in it.

This perspective may make it harder to maintain healthy eating and other habits, which, in turn, leads to lower personal satisfaction and happiness. The end result is a never-ending downward spiral where it becomes almost impossible to be happy.

Researchers now believe that not only is unhappiness unhealthy, but the reverse is also true. Happiness is healthy. A happy and positive outlook on life can significantly reduce heart disease and other diseases caused or exacerbated by stress.

Further, a happy and positive person is more likely to stick to healthy habits and, perhaps, add new habits to reduce stress and its negative impacts on health. Happy people tend to have a "can do" approach to challenges and also have the grit and resiliency to overcome obstacles and disappointments in life.

CHAPTER 2 - IS YOUR FOOD MAKING YOU UNHAPPY?

The food and nutrients we consume have a direct impact on our happiness. First, consumption of too many calories or consumption of unhealthy foods can have a dramatic negative effect on weight and blood pressure. Obesity or weight-related illnesses include: coronary heart disease, including heart attacks and heart failure, strokes, sleep apnea, arthritis, increased risk of certain types of cancer, and high cholesterol. Many of these diseases can lead to a decreased quality of life. Significant health issues and a lowered quality of life can lead to unhappiness.

Obese individuals that live in an area where most of the people are fit or slender, tend to be less happy than fit individuals in the same area and are also less happy than obese or overweight individuals that live in areas with a high percentage of overweight individuals. States with low percentages of overweight individuals include Colorado, California, New York and Massachusetts. States with high percentages of overweight individuals include Mississippi, Michigan, and North Carolina.

Eating well boosts confidence and self-esteem and eating certain foods or types of food can improve mental outlook and reduce anxiety. Referred to as nutritional psychiatry, nutritionists and medical professionals are, in some cases, suggesting dietary changes in lieu of traditional medicine for the treatment of certain mental health issues.

A number of studies have shown that individuals that consume a high percentage of whole foods, including fruits, vegetables, whole grains and unprocessed meats, experienced a lower incidence of anxiety, bipolar disorder and depression when compared to individuals that did not consume as many whole foods. Nutritional psychiatrists think that a similar correlation will exist with other mental health disorders, including dementia and attention deficit disorder.

A diet that is high in unhealthy foods is very likely short on key nutrients that the body needs to properly function. If the brain does not receive proper nutrition, the individual's mood and emotions might be impacted because the brain cells are not functioning the way they should. Nutrition can also impact the way individual genes behave and may increase or decrease a person's genetic predisposition for developing certain conditions or diseases. Nutritional psychiatry also examines the link between the stomach and the brain and the impact poor nutrition has on that relationship. A human stomach lining contains bacteria that keep the stomach and its lining healthy so that it can perform its essential functions. A diet that is abnormally high in certain foods can destroy the lining of the stomach which, in turn, impacts the stomach's ability to synthesize certain mood regulating hormones, such as serotonin and dopamine.

There are certain foods that can be used to boost health and happiness. These foods include foods that are high in Vitamin D, Antioxidants, Omega 3s and foods that support production of serotonin.

What does a "happiness" diet look like? Probably the simplest advice is eat simply and eat cleanly. The old advice to stick to the perimeters of the grocery store is a good rule of thumb for avoiding processed foods which tend to be less beneficial. The fewer things that have been done to the food before it reaches your home the better. For instance, a fresh tomato has been picked, shipped and purchased, whereas canned tomatoes have been picked, processed, heated, sealed, shipped and purchased.

Simple Tips for a Healthier and Happier Diet.

- Limit processed foods and prepare more home cooked meals
- Limit fat intake, particularly saturated fats
- Limit intake of high-fat meat, and increase consumption of lean proteins
- Eat a variety of fruits and vegetables, particularly ones that are colorful
- Eat whole grains when possible
- Increase intake of probiotic foods, including fermented products such as miso and kefir
- limit junk food intake
- Increase intake of Omega-3 rich foods, including certain types of seafood such as salmon, tuna and shrimp
- Avoid trans fats, such as those found in fried foods
 Avoid or limit intake of artificial sweeteners and sugar

- Eat more legumes, which can be a solid replacement for other types of animal-based proteins

 Eat foods rich in Vitamin D, including fortified milk and orange juice, salmon and tuna

- Eat walnuts, hazelnuts and almonds because they are rich in serotonin.

CHAPTER 3 - HOW TO USE EXERCISE TO INCREASE HAPPINESS

As already mentioned above, the way we feel about ourselves can have a significant and determining impact on our view of ourselves and our overall happiness. If a person believes that they are lazy and incompetent, it can become a self-fulfilling prophecy. People that spend their time beating themselves up for their lack of fitness and athletic prowess will not be motivated to hit the gym or go for a walk.

The health benefits of exercise are very well-known; reduced weight, increased muscle and bone mass, higher functioning cardiac and circulatory systems. Exercise reduces the risk of many major health concerns, including heart disease, stroke, diabetes, and osteoporosis. Another major benefit of exercise is that it reduces stress and makes people happier. The euphoria of completing a long run or difficult spinning class or the confidence one gains from being stronger and more fit have a lasting and significant impact on a person's happiness and, by extension, their health.

Exercise increases happiness in a number of ways. First, it reduces stress and anxiety, while at the same time increasing confidence and energy. Exercise also reduces or eliminates insomnia and other sleep difficulties. The science behind exercise-induced happiness is the release of dopamine into the brain. When a person exercises, dopamine is released into the brain. Dopamine is a chemical in the brain that triggers pleasurable and happy feelings. Adhering to a regular exercise program results in the regular release of these "happiness" chemicals into the brain.

In addition to being a happiness strategy all on its own, exercise also plays a part in other happiness tactics discussed in this book. For instance, individuals that exercise will likely be more motivated to maintain healthy eating habits. Exercisers generally sleep more and experience higher quality sleeping patterns. Exercise can also be a great way to add new experiences, spend time outdoors and maintain quality relationships with friends and family, all of which improve a person's overall happiness.

Variety and willingness to try new things is another hallmark of a happy person and exercise is an easy and straightforward way to add new activities. For runners, that may mean adding a yoga class or weightlifting. It's not necessary to become a gym rat or spend hours each day to achieve an increase in fitness and happiness. Let's face it - not everyone has the time or the desire to spend a good part of each week grinding it out on a treadmill or in an exercise class.

The good news is that shorter exercise periods can yield the same health benefits of more traditional fitness programs. High Intensity Interval Training (HIIT) has been shown to improve health, fitness and happiness using short bursts of extremely intense exercises. As little as a few minutes a day may be enough to get that dopamine burst that tells your brain how happy it is.

CHAPTER 4 - GET A GOOD NIGHT'S SLEEP AND BE HAPPY ALL DAY.

Anyone who has stayed up too late with a sick child or binge-watching on Netflix, can tell you that lack of sleep leads to fuzzy thinking, slower reactions and grumpiness. What is less well known is that a chronic lack of adequate sleep can have significant health consequences, including cardiac issues and high blood pressure.

Lack of sleep also leads to memory loss, which means it might not even be possible to remember what it feels like to wake up refreshed and ready for the day. Sleep-deprived people also tend to eat more and eat unhealthily because a lack of sleep interferes with the hormones in your body that trigger when to eat and when not to eat.

A lack of sleep causes the appetite suppressing hormone, leptin, to decrease, while at the same time telling the hormone that triggers eating, ghrelin, to increase. To make matters worse, ghrelin is manufactured by the body's fat cells and it signals the body that it needs to consume more fat. An increase in ghrelin tells your body to eat more, which in turn may make more fat cells, which - you guessed it- will produce more ghrelin telling you to eat more fat.

Plain and simple - lack of sleep makes people unhappy and unhealthy. That's easy to understand, but as anyone who has spent a night tossing and turning can tell you, sleeping is easier said than done. Thankfully, there are a number of tips and strategies that people can implement to make falling asleep, and staying asleep, a little easier. These strategies include:

Limit all screen time a few hours before bedtime. Using a computer or iPad, and even watching television, may interfere with the brain's ability to shut down in preparation of sleep. Falling asleep with the television on is an particularly bad habit because, as your body cycles through its normal sleep patterns, the sound and lights from the television may cause a person to wake up and be unable to fall back to sleep.

Be mindful of food and beverages consumed prior to bedtime. Being hungry or stuffed to the gills at bedtime can make falling asleep more difficult. If your mind is consumed with how hungry it is or how uncomfortably full it is, it will be more difficult for the mind and body to fall asleep. Limiting beverages of all kinds prior to bed is another good sleep strategy because it helps to eliminate the urge to wake up to go to the bathroom. Particular items that should be avoided prior to bed include alcohol, spicy food, caffeine and nicotine because each of these may make it more difficult to fall asleep or may interfere with the body's sleep rhythms.

For example, while alcohol may make it easier to fall asleep, it is also likely to interfere with sleep later in the night. A light bedtime snack may make it easier to fall asleep, particularly if it contains carbohydrates and a little protein containing tryptophan (e.g., turkey).

Develop a sleep schedule and sleep rituals. To make falling asleep easier, it is beneficial to have an established sleep schedule, which means people should go to bed and wake up at approximately the same time every day, including holidays and vacations. Establishing a pre-bed ritual, such as reading or gentle stretching, signals the mind and body that it is time to go to bed. The right sleeping environment is also helpful in getting a good night's sleep. A comfortable bed in a quiet room that is cool and dark is the ideal sleeping environment.

In addition to these tactics, exercise and reduced stress can also lead to a better night's sleep. In addition to encouraging a good night's sleep, increasing exercise and reducing stress are also important strategies in becoming a happier person.

Surroundings Can Have an Important Impact on Happiness.

For instance, people that spend time outdoors tend to be happier than people who have limited time in nature. Work environments can be engineered to increase employee happiness and productivity. Also, the psychological reaction to certain colors has been used by business and marketers for years to modify consumer behavior.

The Importance of Nature.

Recent studies have shown a correlation between people's happiness and how connected they felt to nature. In one study, children who learned in outdoor classrooms showed significantly improved scores compared to their results while learning in a traditional classroom environment. One study, conducted in the United Kingdom, followed a small group of individuals some of whom moved from an urban environment to a greener, more natural environment and some of whom moved from a greener environment to a more urban environment.

After three years, the study showed that the participants who moved to the more natural environment experienced increased happiness that the other group. The fact of being in a natural environment results in increased energy and more positive feelings, which, in turn, lead to a more optimistic and happier outlook on life. It is not necessary to move to a farm or other rural area to experience the happiness boost associated with nature. Simple things, like walking through the park on your way to work or cultivating a patio garden or indoor plants can also yield a significant increase in happiness.

Spending time outdoors also increases the skin's production of Vitamin D, a vitamin that has many health benefits, including prevention of cancer and autoimmune diseases. Vitamin D also enhances happiness and a person's overall sense of well-being by improving sleep and reducing depression.

Creating a Happy Work Environment.

As much as we wish it weren't true, the majority of us spend a great deal of time at work. Whether we work in a traditional work environment or from our home, there are steps we can all take to inject a little nature and happiness into our work environment. An obvious step is decorating our offices with plants, pictures of loved ones and mementos of past achievements and positive experiences.

While everyone is going to have a bad day at work, it is possible to have an overall feeling of happiness and accomplishment by following a few small steps.

First, bookend your day with positivity. By truly savoring your morning cup of coffee or tea and by reflecting on the day's accomplishments and positive developments before you leave, you create an overall sense of competency and joy in your position. It is also important to take advantage of opportunities to move and interact with co-workers. Of course, it is quicker and easier to email a colleague with a question, but every now and then stopping by and asking the question in person can lead to a happier work environment. First, it provides a quick burst of physical activity, which we know leads to increased happiness. Second, it provides a little personal interaction that is also known to increase happiness. Reducing work stress is another way to create a happy work environment. De-cluttering a desk, creating and sticking to a to-do list can relieve some of the day-in and day-out stress of work.

Surround Yourself with Happy Colors.

Have you ever wondered why most fast food restaurants rely on the color red as their main decorating accent? It's because the color red heightens activity, increases appetite and encourages impulse reactions. Similarly, colors can be used to soothe and relax people.

Happy colors include: blue, green, pink, orange, and surprisingly, brown. Colors that may spur negative or unhappy feelings include: black, red, purple, and in some instances, yellow and white. Blue is a relaxing color that lowers blood pressure, reduces appetite and leads to an overall sense of calm and security. Associated with cleanliness, the color green has been shown to alleviate pain and promote optimism and happiness. Similarly, pink and orange are colors that inspire happy or relaxed feelings. Interestingly, while most people wouldn't choose brown as a "happy" color, it does promote feelings of comfort and coziness, which, in turn, lead to reduced stress and increased happiness.

In addition to the excitement and frenetic action caused by the color red, the color yellow also inspires feelings of strong negative emotion. Over long periods of time, the color yellow can cause angry or hostile feelings and outbursts. One caveat to this generalization is that, in limited doses, the color yellow can invoke feelings of happiness and friendliness. So a bit of yellow, perhaps on an accent pillow or as one color in a pattern, may add a dose of happy feelings into a room. The colors purple and white, are not clear-cut as "happy" or "sad" colors. A purple color scheme may encourage creativity but it may also trigger mournfulness.

Similarly, the color white, which is associated with cleanliness, can in some situations be so bland as to trigger feelings of emptiness. Further, in some cultures, white is the color of death or mourning. For most people, the color most frequently associated with death is black and, for that reason, it is generally not a color that triggers happy feelings.

Chapter 6. Attitude is Everything - At Least When it Comes to Happiness.

Scientists believe that happiness is driven almost equally by genetic and environmental influences. This does mean that some people have a genetic predisposition toward unhappiness. However, being predisposed to a gloomy outlook does not mean that happiness is an unattainable goal. In fact, unlike most genetic predispositions, a positive outlook can alter your genetic predisposition.

On the other hand, persons that have a genetic predisposition for happiness can become downers if their environment and life choices tend to focus on negative and unhappy things. So whether you were born an Eeyore or a Tigger, attitude is everything when it comes to maintaining a sunny disposition and living a happy life. There are a number of actions that can be taken to have a positive and happy attitude.

Get Rid of Negative Thoughts.

That nagging inner voice that constantly criticizes and finds fault with everything that you do can do a number on happiness. It's hard to have a cheery outlook when someone is constantly highlighting your flaws. People with positive attitudes find a way to silence their inner critic. The use of positive affirmations on a regular or as-needed basis can help erase negative thoughts that lead to unhappiness.

Affirmations can be directed towards building self-esteem and confidence and can help create a new thought process in the person's psyche. Affirmations can also be goal oriented towards success or health or weight loss. For people with particularly, loud and stubborn inner critics, it can be helpful to physically manifest the negative thoughts that are leading to unhappiness.

These thoughts can then be erased, thrown away, burned or otherwise discarded. Further, writing down happy experiences and positive achievements can improve an individual's happiness. By erasing negative thoughts and replacing them with positive thoughts, it is possible to improve one's attitude and zest for living.

Be Creative.

Allowing your mind to wander can have many benefits, one of which is increased happiness. A creative and wandering mind can help find answers or explanations for problems or challenges. Using your imagination to overcome an imagined obstacle can lead to confidence in overcoming real-life obstacles. Resiliency and the ability to rebound from disappointments is a cornerstone of a happy life.

Meditate or do Yoga.

Sometimes detaching from one's life is an important part of the happiness process. There are many health benefits associated with meditation and yoga and living a more happy life is just one of them. Many people find it difficult to quiet the mind and body to achieve the full benefits of meditation and yoga. However, there are a number of different types of meditation that may be helpful in getting a regular meditation practice started. A few of the different types of meditation involve some form of movement because many people aren't comfortable sitting in one spot for an extended period of time. For those people, standing, walking or dance meditation may be more enjoyable. There are also a number of mediation programs or classes, such as tai chi, that people who want to be in a group setting may enjoy.

Don't Harbor Grudges; Let Some Things Go.

Thinking that everything has to go a certain way or keeping an ongoing mental tally of every slight, snub or resentment is almost certain to lead to unhappiness. Further, thinking that every little decision has to be made by you, either at work or at home, can be overwhelming and can also diminish happiness. To live a happy life, it is imperative that people forgive past slights and arguments and move forward. It is also important to forgive ourselves for past mistakes or failures.

Be a Realistic Optimist.

Optimists see the best in everything, the world is their oyster and there is no hurdle they can't climb. In some instances, optimists just believe things will work out the way they are supposed to. Having an optimistic outlook releases a great deal of pressure and makes it easier to have a happy and positive outlook on life. It is important to temper the optimism with a realistic approach to the world and its problems. Blind optimism that is not based on any realistic approach or result can lead to unexpected disappointments, which, in turn, may lead to unhappiness.

Chapter 7 - The Impact of Relationships on Happiness.

Who we surround ourselves with may have as much to do with our individual happiness as any other factor. While we can all agree that bad relationships - who hasn't had at least one of those - can make us unhappy and that good relationships can make us happier, the relation between relationships and happiness is a little more complicated than that. Of course, surrounding ourselves with happy, positive and supportive people that love and respect us is a great first step. Equally important is the need to eliminate toxic people from our lives.

Many people make the mistake of assuming that the life of the party - the person with 100 friends - is by definition happy. That may or may not be true. It is the quality of our relationships, and not the quantity of them, that determines whether or not an individual is happy.

Studies have found that individuals with a network of acquaintances can be happy so long as they have at least one close relationship. A relationship was classified as a "close relationship" if the individuals were comfortable revealing close, personal and intimate details about their life. On the other hand, an individual with a wide array of friends who does not deeply share their life is likely to experience feelings of loneliness and isolation.

What is important in determining happiness as it pertains to relationships is that feeling of being known and understood; like someone "gets" you and acts as a witness to your life with all its feelings. In addition to close relationships with friends, having a strong and low-stress marriage and a network of work friends are also important in achieving happiness. As happy as it makes us to have someone give their friendship to us, happiness is equally tied to the benefits we experience from giving friendship, support and loyalty to another person.

Chapter 8 - Being a Little Selfish Might Be the Key to Happiness

Recharging is an important component of happiness. Individuals that constantly give of themselves and do not take time for themselves report a higher incidence of unhappiness. By carving time out of our schedule to put ourselves first we are telling ourselves that we are important and meaningful.

Simple things like getting a massage or haircut can rejuvenate our spirit and increase our happiness and positive outlook on life. Failure to care for our emotional and physical health can lead to illness, depression and overall unhappiness.

To feel the most happy, it is important to take time each day to treat yourself. Simply waiting around and doing one big day once a year will likely not have the positive impact on happiness that smaller, more regular treats will have. For people with demanding jobs or a busy family life, it can be difficult to carve time out on a daily basis, but it will pay dividends in happiness, which will result in being a better and more productive employee and a more patient and loving spouse and parent.

In addition to beauty treatments, recharging can also be done while out on a walk, reading a book, listening to music, going for a car or motorcycle ride.

CHAPTER 9 - BUT NOT TOO SELFISH - HOW GIVING MAKES PEOPLE HAPPY

We've all heard the adage that "it is better to give than to receive." It turns out that, with respect to happiness, that old adage may have a ring of truth to it. As a general rule, people are happier when they feel needed, appreciated and like their life and work matters.

While in a previous chapter, we said that it's necessary to put yourself first sometimes in order to be happy, the key part of that sentence is "sometimes." When people become hyper focused on themselves, their accomplishments and their needs, they lose perspective of what life is really about.

The fact of giving back, either through donation of time or money, ties people to a bigger picture.

CHAPTER 10 - ADD A FURRY OR FINNED FRIEND TO YOUR LIFE

One only needs to look at the proliferation of kitten and puppy images on Instagram to know that we love our pets. Maybe the reason for the love is that domesticated animals provide one of the purest forms of unconditional love there is. No matter what you look like, how much money you make, or how boring your personality is - to your pet, you're the best thing on two legs.

Perhaps it is that feeling of love and total acceptance that makes owning a pet one of the most effective means of increasing happiness. The increased use of therapy dogs for the elderly and sick children shows how a snuggle from a furry friend can release stress and put a smile of happiness on even the saddest of faces.

Scientific and anecdotal evidence clearly show that relationships with pets provide significant emotional support that lead to increased happiness in pet owners. Further, studies have shown that pet owners are, as a general rule, happier than non-pet owners and that the happiness benefits achieved from close friendships can be replicated by ownership of a pet.

What makes these results more interesting is that people who gain the most from human relationships seem to experience a compounding effect when it comes to happiness gains resulting from pet ownership.

Recent studies conducted by specialists in cardiac care show that ownership of pets, particularly dogs, reduce the risk of high blood pressure and heart disease. Certain studies have shown that dog ownership can significantly reduce blood pressure in individuals that have previously shown elevated blood pressure levels.

One of the main benefits of dog ownership is the release of pleasure hormones, dopamine and serotonin, that result from playing and cuddling with pets. Further, the cholesterol levels of dog owners are measurably lower than he levels of persons who do not own pets.

Interestingly, the type of pet does not matter when looking at happiness in owners. While everyone can understand the happiness garnered from ownership of a cute and cuddly puppy, it appears that similar happiness gains can be achieved even in the least cuddly of pets. It's not the type of pet that matters so much as the owner's emotional connection to that pet.

Why is pet ownership so important?

In addition to encouraging a loving relationship, pet ownership can encourage certain healthy habits, including exercise. Pet ownership also provides friendship or companionship and can break the ice when meeting new people.

CHAPTER 11 - HOW KEEPING UP WITH THE JONESES CAN LEAD TO UNHAPPINESS.

Unfortunately, many people judge their success by material possessions. What car they drive or what their zip code is becomes more important than the type of person they are or how they make others feel. Keeping score based on possessions can lead to feelings of failure when people compare what they have to what others have. It's hard to feel happy when you feel like a failure.

Another significant downside to this way of thinking is the financial stress and strain that can result from the constant need to keep up with society's perception of what is deemed "successful." To make matters worse, it has been shown time and time again that possessions don't lead to happiness. Rather it's relationships and experiences that ultimately lead to happiness.

The stress associated with strained finances can lead to heart problems, strokes, migraines and other chronic headaches, ulcers, high blood pressure and poor sleeping patterns. It's not hard to see that with any one or more of these ailments, it will be difficult to maintain a happy life. Exacerbating the health risks and unhappiness associated with financial stress is the fact that many people adopt coping mechanisms such as alcohol or drug abuse or overeating to take their minds off the stress.

As noted above, each of these in and of itself can be a barrier to happiness. Also, financial strain is one of the most frequent grounds cited as the reason a couple divorces. The loss of this relationship will likely have a significant negative impact on an individual's happiness.

To increase happiness, it can be helpful to limit or eliminate as much financial stress as possible. The first step in accomplishing this is creating and sticking to a realistic budget. The budget needs to provide for the payment of current necessary expenses as well as long- and short-term savings for unexpected expenses as well as for retirement. A realistic budget may necessitate certain sacrifices that may sting initially, but will pay dividends in the future as the individual reduces their financial stress and increases their level of happiness.

The ironic thing about financial stress is that, when you ask most people about what makes them happy, they rarely respond in a way that shows they value possessions. Rather, what makes people happy is their relationships with family and friends and the experiences they have had during their lifetime.

Studies have shown that the amount of money an individual has is not nearly as important to their overall happiness as is how they spend their money. For instance, people that use their money to help others or to experience new things are significantly happier than individuals who spend their money on expensive cars, homes and other "possessions."

Unfortunately, many people feel that splurging on a vacation or Broadway show does not make as much monetary sense as buying a nice car. The rationale is that when the experience is over, the person will have nothing to show for what they spent. At least with a car or other possession, they have "something" to show for their money. However, when people reflect back on their expenditures and what purchases made them happiest, it is most likely an expense associated with an experience that made them the most happy. It appears that the memory of a trip or other experience is far more fulfilling and sustaining than a memory of a particularly expensive handbag purchase.

One study showed that study participants routinely predicted that purchasing "something" would be more valuable than purchasing an experience. However, after the event or purchase, the individuals that purchased an experience exhibited significantly higher happiness than individuals who had purchased "something."

Spending money on experiences instead of "things" is beneficial to happiness in other ways as well. First, experiences tend to be experienced with other people leading to better relationships with family and friends or a closer connection to the world at large. Second, it is more difficult to and people tend to not indulge in comparing experiences to the experiences of others.

While someone might look envyingly at a neighbors new boat, that same feeling of envy does not exist with respect to experiences because the value of the experience is our memories and the feelings the experience invoked. Those emotions are hard to quantify and compare.

Another way that purchasing experiences increases happiness is that thinking about an upcoming vacation or romantic dinner is far more pleasurable than thinking about the fancy car you are going to buy next month. So in addition to experiences making people happier after the acquisition, it also appears that purchasing experiences makes people happier before the expenditure too.

CONCLUSION

Being happy and optimistic can positively impact a person's overall health and well-being. Furthermore, it is human instinct to want to achieve a sense of happiness.

Why is it easier for some people to achieve a state of happiness?

The primary reason lies in the fact that like eye color, a predisposition to happiness is genetically predetermined. However, unlike eye color and other inherited characteristics, what we want is almost as important as what our genetics dictate.

When it comes to happiness, people that want to be happy or that choose happiness, can honestly be happy if they follow a few simple strategies.

Health is a driving force in human happiness, so persons that eat right, exercise and get the right amount of sleep should be happier and more content than their counterparts with shoddy habits.

Our happiness is also manageable. We can improve our happiness by managing our environment and attitude. Further, by avoiding certain stresses, including financial and relationship stress, individuals can positively impact the amount of happiness they experience on a daily basis.

Made in the USA
San Bernardino, CA
14 February 2017